JUDY CRAYMER, RICHARD EAST AND BJÖRN ULVAEUS FOR LITTLESTAR
IN ASSOCIATION WITH UNIVERSAL PRESENT

MAMMA MIA!

MUSIC AND LYRICS BY
BENNY ANDERSSON
BJÖRN ULVAEUS
AND SOME SONGS WITH STIG ANDERSON

BOOK BY CATHERINE JOHNSON

PRODUCTION DESIGNED BY
MARK THOMPSON

LIGHTING DESIGNED BY
HOWARD HARRISON

SOUND DESIGNED BY
ANDREW BRUCE & BOBBY AITKEN

MUSICAL SUPERVISOR
ADDITIONAL MATERIAL & ARRANGEMENTS
MARTIN KOCH

CHOREOGRAPHY
ANTHONY VAN LAAST

DIRECTED BY
PHYLLIDA LLOYD

D1287764

Project Manager: Carol Cuellar
Book Art Layout: Joe Klucar

"ABBA-SOLUTELY fabulous!"

London Daily Mail   New York Newsday   Toronto Star   Melbourne Herald Sun

"It's great to be having fun at the theatre again! The riotously infectious MAMMA MIA! is one of the brightest, funniest musicals playing anywhere in the world right now. Phyllida Lloyd's meticulous production is a key ingredient of the success, and Catherine Johnson's book, accomplished with wit and warmth, lovingly embraces the ABBA songs to fashion an original story into which 22 hits are perfectly dovetailed."

Mark Shenton, BBC

"A sensation! Just sit back and let the joy sweep over you!"

Clive Barnes, New York Post

"Perhaps the single most ecstatic musical to open on Broadway since 'A Chorus Line'! MAMMA MIA! leaves you uplifted, enraptured and feeling like a number one!"

Owen Gleiberman, Entertainment Weekly

"Fabulous, funny and endlessly clever, it brilliantly weaves those familiar ABBA songs into the plot. If you can get a ticket, you'll love it!"

T. R. Reid, Washington Post

Louise Pitre

Paul Basleigh, Raza Jaffrey and Adam C. Booth

Louise Gold, Lesley Nicol and Louise Plowright

Tina Maddigan and Adam Brazier

CONTENTS

Louise Pitre

DANCING QUEEN

Words and Music by
BENNY ANDERSSON, STIG ANDERSON
and BJÖRN ULVAEUS

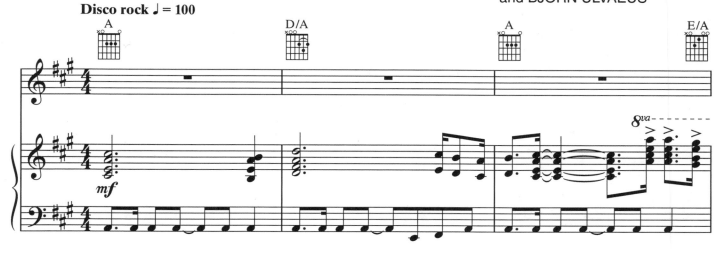

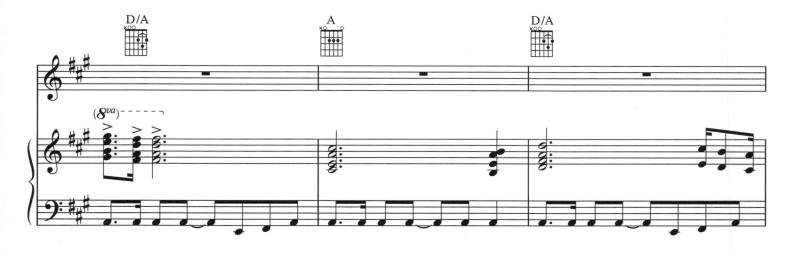

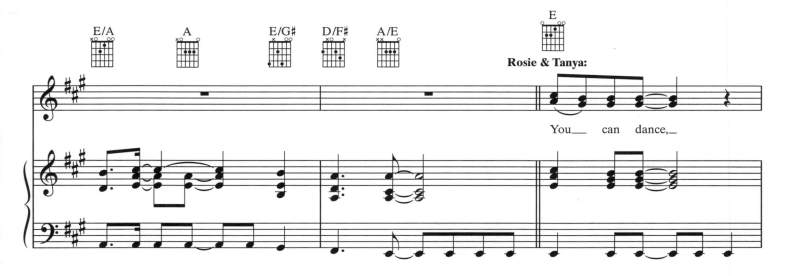

Dancing Queen - 7 - 1
PFM0205

10

Verse 1:

1. Fri - day night_ and the lights are low,_

Chorus:

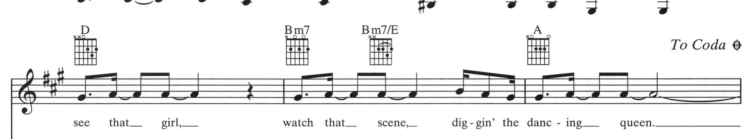

having the time of your life. Ooh,

see that girl, watch that scene, dig-gin' the danc-ing queen.

To Coda ⊕

D.S. ℅ al Coda

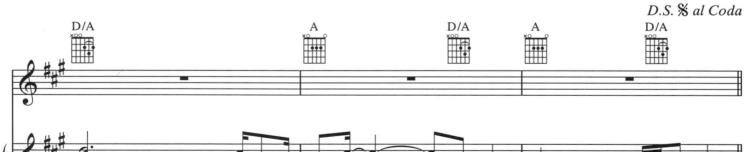

VOULEZ-VOUS

Words and Music by
BENNY ANDERSSON
and BJÖRN ULVAEUS

Voulez-vous - 8 - 2
PFM0205

18

Chorus:

19

To Coda

And here we
go a - gain,__ we know the start,__ we know the end.__ Mas-ters of the scene.__
We've done it all be-fore__ and now we're back__ to get some more.__

Voulez-vous - 8 - 4
PFM0205

20

CHIQUITITA

Words and Music by
BENNY ANDERSSON
and BJÖRN ULVAEUS

Freely, with feeling

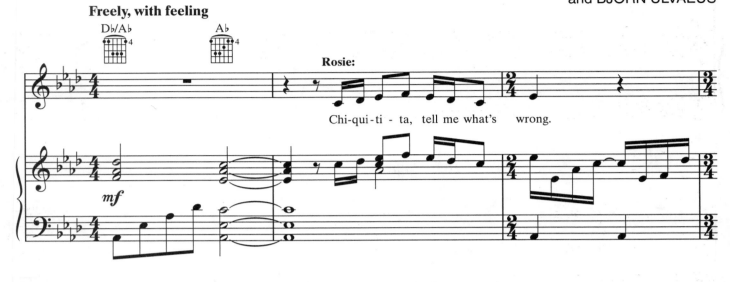

Rosie:
Chi-qui-ti - ta, tell me what's wrong.

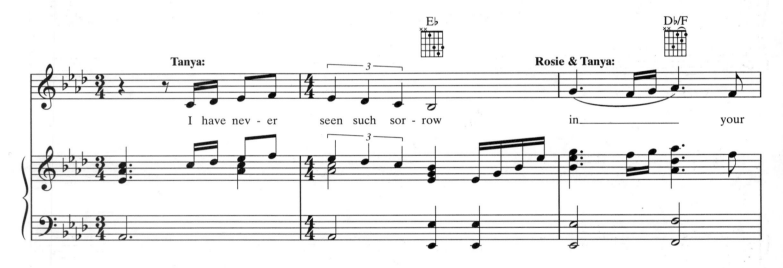

Tanya:
I have nev - er seen such sor - row

Rosie & Tanya:
in _____ your

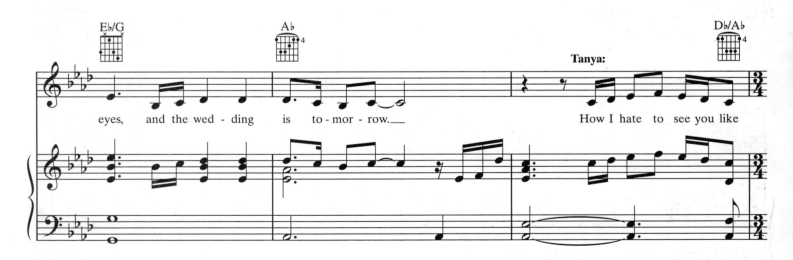

eyes, and the wed - ding is to - mor - row. ___

Tanya:
How I hate to see you like

Chiquitita - 5 - 1
PFM0205

26

must re - ly___ on.___ You were al - ways sure of your - self.

Now I see you've bro - ken a feath - er.___

I___ hope we can patch___ it up

to - geth - er.___ Chi - qui - ti - ta, you and I___

28

Chiquitita - 5 - 5
PFM0205

THANK YOU FOR THE MUSIC

Words and Music by
BENNY ANDERSSON
and BJÖRN ULVAEUS

GIMME! GIMME! GIMME!
(A Man After Midnight)

Words and Music by
BENNY ANDERSSON
and BJÖRN ULVAEUS

Girl Ensemble:

Is there a man out there?

Some-one to hear my prayer?

Gimme! Gimme! Gimme! - 8 - 1
PFM0205

Dm
Harry: Is your dad here?
Sophie: I don't know.
Harry: What?
Sophie: I don't know who my dad is.
cresc.
B♭6
Gm6
Is there a man out__ there?__
Some-one to hear my__ prayer?__
mf
A7
Dm
Bill: Can I be nosy? I'm a writer, so it goes with the territory.
Sophie: Go on.
p
3
3

40

LAY ALL YOUR LOVE ON ME

Words and Music by
BENNY ANDERSSON
and BJÖRN ULVAEUS

Disco rock ♩ = 132
Verse 1:

44

48

SUPER TROUPER

Words and Music by
BENNY ANDERSSON
and BJÖRN ULVAEUS

Moderately ♩=120

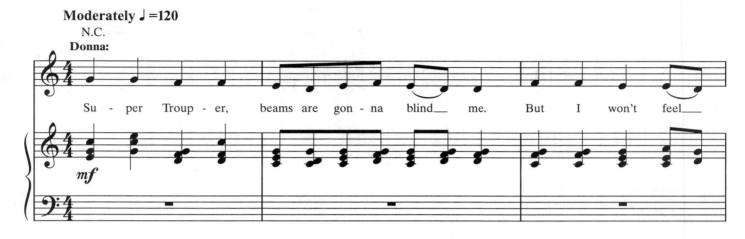

Su - per Troup - er, beams are gon - na blind__ me. But I won't feel__

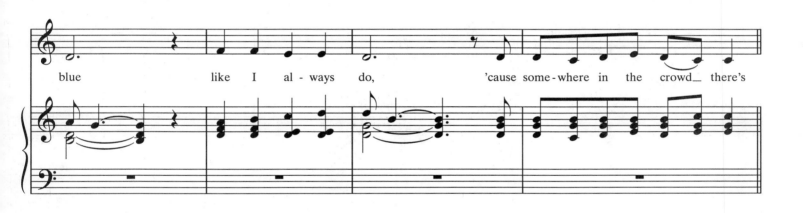

blue like I al - ways do, 'cause some - where in the crowd__ there's

you.

Super Trouper - 5 - 1
PFM0205

Verse:

1. I was sick and tired of ev-'ry-thing when I called___ you last night from
2. Fac-ing twen-ty thou-sand of your friends, how can an-y-one be so

Glas - gow. All I do is eat and drink and sing, wish-ing ev-
lone - ly? Part of a suc-cess that nev-er ends, still I'm think-

'ry show was the last_____ show. So i-mag-ine I was
ing a-bout you on - ly. There are mo-ments when I

51

Super Trouper - 5 - 3
PFM0205

MONEY, MONEY, MONEY

Words and Music by
BENNY ANDERSSON
and BJÖRN ULVAEUS

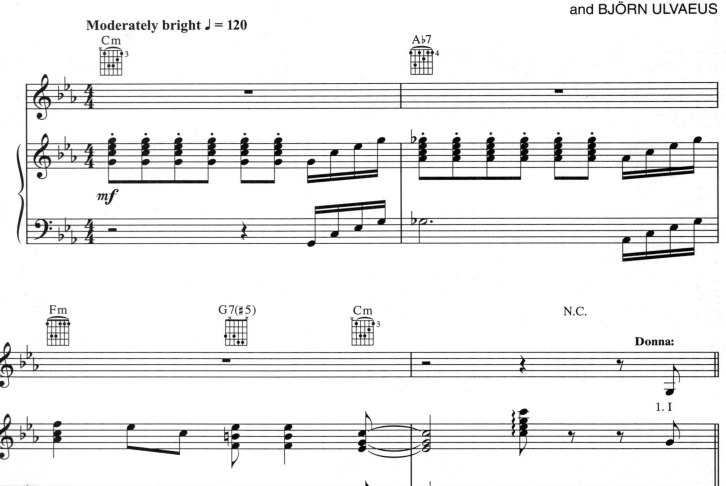

Moderately bright ♩ = 120

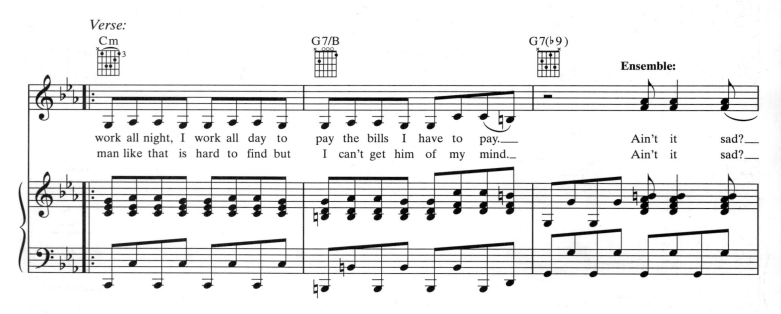

work all night, I work all day to pay the bills I have to pay.___ Ain't it sad?___

man like that is hard to find but I can't get him of my mind.___ Ain't it sad?___

Money, Money, Money - 6 - 1
PFM0205

56

57

Money, Money, Money - 6 - 4
PFM0205

58

Money, Money, Money - 6 - 5
PFM0205

MAMMA MIA

Words and Music by
BENNY ANDERSSON, STIG ANDERSON
and BJÖRN ULVAEUS

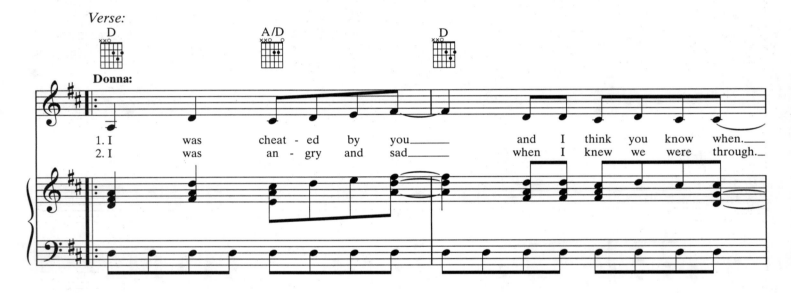

1. I was cheat-ed by you___ and I think you know when.___
2. I was an-gry and sad___ when I knew we were through.___

63

should not have let you go.

should not have let you go.

Donna: *What the hell are you all doing here? Well, I'd love to stop and chat, but I have to go and clean out my handbag or something.*

Bill: *Age does not wither her.*

Harry: *I was expecting a rather stout matron.*

HONEY, HONEY

Words and Music by
BENNY ANDERSSON, BJÖRN ULVAEUS
and STIG ANDERSON

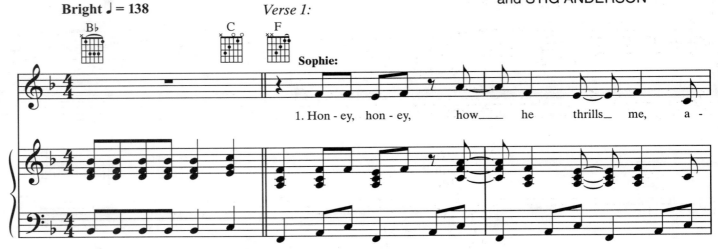

Honey, Honey - 6 - 1
PFM0205

Verse 2:

F
Hon - ey, hon - ey, don't con - ceal it, a -
B♭
ha, hon - ey, hon - ey. The
F
way that you kiss good night,
Dm
the
The way that you kiss me good -
F
way that you hold me tight.
Dm
I
night,
the way that you're hold - ing me

70

No, they think my mum sent the invitations —

and after reading this diary I'm not surprised they all said yes!

Verse 3:

Hon - ey, hon - ey, how___ you thrill___ me, a - ha, hon - ey, hon - ey.

Hon - ey, hon - ey, near - ly kill___ me, a -

THE NAME OF THE GAME

Words and Music by
BENNY ANDERSSON, STIG ANDERSON
and BJÖRN ULVAEUS

74

S.O.S.

Words and Music by
BENNY ANDERSSON, BJÖRN ULVAEUS
and STIG ANDERSON

S.O.S. - 7 - 1
PFM0205

UNDER ATTACK

Words and Music by
BENNY ANDERSSON
and BJÖRN ULVAEUS

Moderate techno ♩=116

1. Don't know how to take it, don't know____ where to go,____ my re-sis-tance run-ning low.____
2. *See additional lyrics*

Under Attack - 5 - 1
PFM0205

Coda

would know___ how._____

Verse 2:
This is getting crazy, I should tell them so,
Really let my anguish show.
I feel like I was trapped within a nightmare,
I've got nowhere to go.
(Still undecided, I suppose.)
Yes, it's what I wanted but I'm scared as hell,
Staring down the deepest well.
I hardly dare to think of what would happen,
Where I'd be if I fell:
(To Chorus:)

DOES YOUR MOTHER KNOW

Words and Music by
BENNY ANDERSSON
and BJÖRN ULVAEUS

Moderately fast ♩ = 136

N.C.

mf

Verse:

Bb   Gm   Bb

Tanya:

1. You're so hot___ teas - ing me.___ So you're blue,___
2. I can see___ what you want.___ But you seem___

Eb   Bb/D   Cm7   Bb   F

___ but I can't take a chance on a kid like you,___
___ pret - ty young to be search - ing for that kind of fun,

Chorus:

dance with you, hon-ey, if_____ you think it's fun-ny, does___

_____ your moth-er know that you're out?_____ And I could

chat with you, ba-by, flirt_____ a lit-tle may-be, does___

_____ your moth-er know that you're out?_____ Take it

96

D.S. ℅ al Coda

moth - er   know?___

Well, I could

OUR LAST SUMMER

Words and Music by
BENNY ANDERSSON
and BJÖRN ULVAEUS

Chorus:

our __ last sum - mer. I still __ see it all, _____

__ in the tour - ist jam, round the No - tre Dame. __ Our __ last

sum - mer, __ walk - ing hand in hand. Par - is res - tau - rants, __ our __ last

sum - mer, __ morn - ing crois - sants. _____ Liv - ing for the day, __

you were the he - ro of my dreams._____ I can still re - call

_____ our last sum - mer.__ I can see it all,_____

_____ walks a - long the Seine, laugh - ing in the rain.__

_____ Our last sum - mer,__ mem - 'ries that re - call.

rit. e dim.

THE WINNER TAKES IT ALL

Words and Music by
BENNY ANDERSSON
and BJÖRN ULVAEUS

now_____ it's his - to - ry.
build - ing me a fence,
when_____ she calls your name?
you've come to shake my hand.

I've_____ played all my cards
build - ing me a home,
Some - where deep in - side,
I_____ a - pol - o - gize

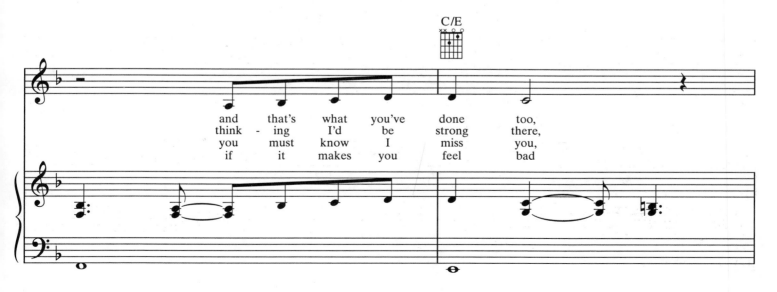

and that's what you've done too,
think - ing I'd be strong there,
you must know I miss you,
if it makes you feel bad

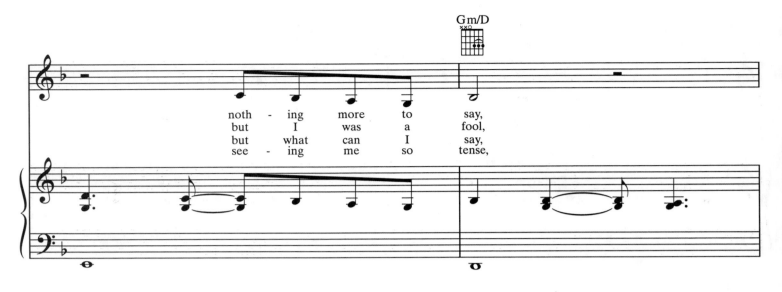

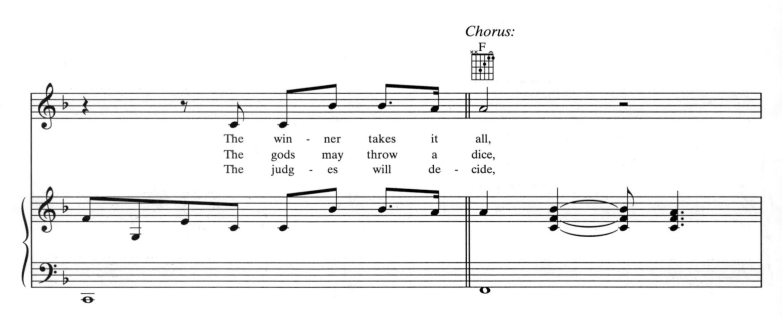

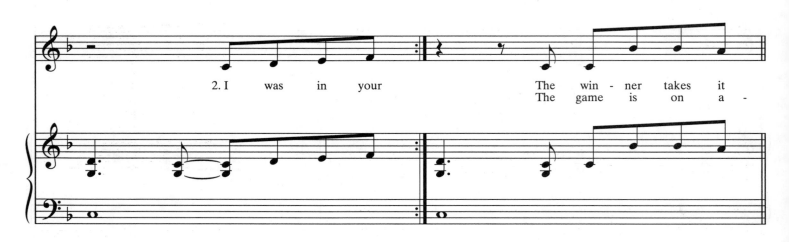

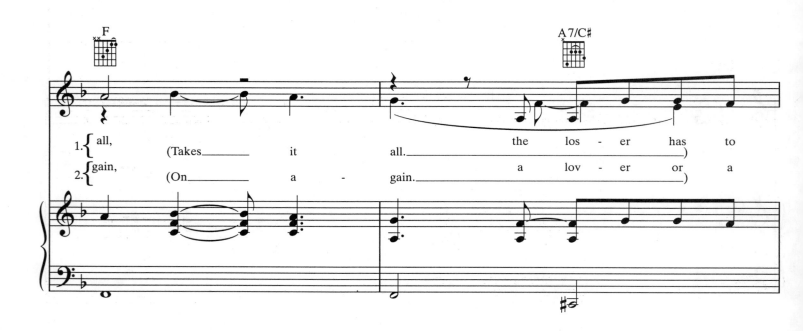

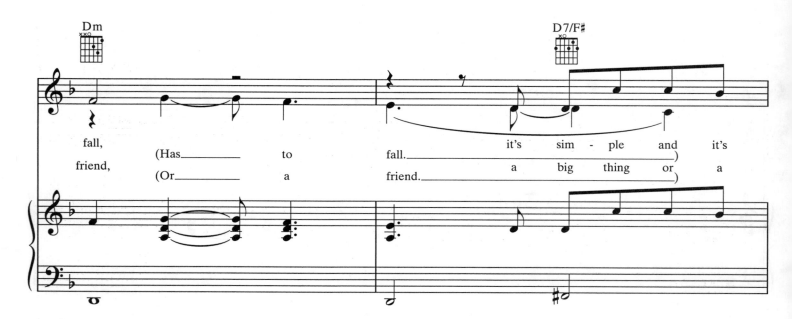

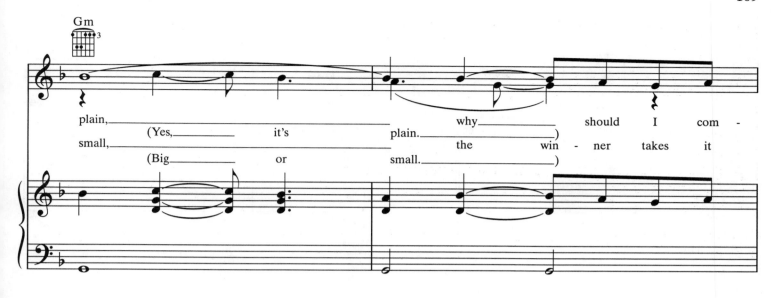

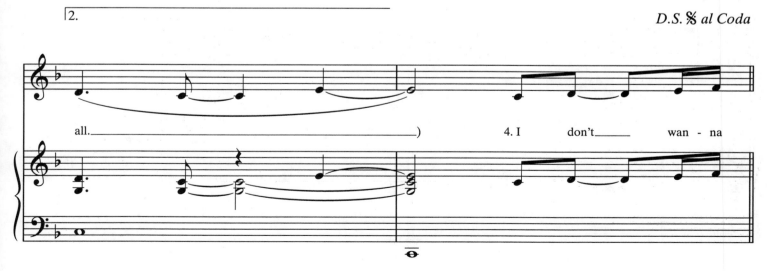

D.S. 𝄋 al Coda

The Winner Takes It All - 8 - 6
PFM0205

110

ONE OF US

Words and Music by
BENNY ANDERSSON
and BJÖRN ULVAEUS

One of us is lone-ly, one of us is on-ly wait-ing for a call,_____ sor-ry for her-self, feel-ing stu-pid, feel-ing small, wish-ing you had nev-er left at all.

One of Us - 4 - 1
PFM0205

Chorus:

I HAVE A DREAM

Words and Music by
BENNY ANDERSSON
and BJÖRN ULVAEUS

Moderately ♩ = 104

1. I have a

dream,   a   song   to   sing   to   help   me

Verse 2:

dream, a fan - ta - sy to help me through_____ re - al - i - ty. And my des - ti - na - tion_____ makes it worth the while,_____ push - ing through the dark - ness,_____

120

TAKE A CHANCE ON ME

Words and Music by
BENNY ANDERSSON
and BJÖRN ULVAEUS

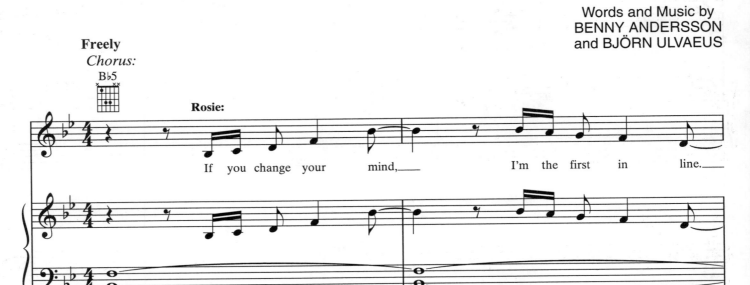

Take a Chance on Me - 9 - 1
PFM0205

Chorus:

If you change your mind,____ I'm the first in line.____

Hon - ey, I'm still free,____ take a chance on me.____

If you need me, let____ me know, gon - na be a - round,__

____ if you've got no place____ to go when you're

130

I DO, I DO, I DO, I DO, I DO

Words and Music by
BENNY ANDERSSON, BJÖRN ULVAEUS
and STIG ANDERSON

KNOWING ME, KNOWING YOU

Words and Music by
BENNY ANDERSSON, STIG ANDERSON
and BJÖRN ULVAEUS

Chorus:

SLIPPING THROUGH MY FINGERS

Words and Music by
BENNY ANDERSSON
and BJÖRN ULVAEUS

Moderately slow ♩ = 70
Verse:

Donna:

1. School - bag in hand,___ she leaves home___ in the ear - ly morn - ing,
2. Sleep in our eyes,___ her and me___ at the break - fast ta - ble,

(with pedal)

wav - ing good - bye___ wtih an ab - sent - mind - ed smile.___
bare - ly a - wake,___ I let pre - cious time go by.___

I watch her go, with a surge___
Then when she's gone, there's that old___

144

Slipping Through My Fingers - 5 - 5
PFM0205